MW01075660

Christian Life & Witness Course

A four-part study that will help
Christians revitalize their own
faith and share it with others.

The Christian Life and Witness Course was originally prepared by Charlie Riggs, Director of the Counseling and Follow-Up Department for the Billy Graham Evangelistic Association from 1957 to 1989.

Christian Life and Witness Course

© 1979, 1990, 1998 Billy Graham Evangelistic Association

Published by World Wide Publications
1303 Hennepin Avenue
Minneapolis, Minnesota 55403

Unless otherwise noted, Scripture quotations are from the *Holy Bible, New International Version.* Copyright © 1973, 1978, 1984 International Bible Society. Used by permission of Zondervan Bible Publishers.

Scripture quotations marked NKJV are taken from the *Holy Bible, New King James Version.* Copyright © 1979, 1980, 1982 by Thomas Nelson, Inc. Nashville, Tennessee.

ISBN 0-89066-299-1

Printed in U.S.A.

Preface

For over 45 years the Christian Life and Witness Course has been taught all over the world in preparation for Crusades sponsored by the Billy Graham Evangelistic Association. As a result, thousands of Christians have been renewed in their relationship with Jesus Christ and equipped to effectively share their faith with others in both daily life and as counselors during the Crusade.

It is our prayer that as a result of taking this course you would have a fresh sense of God at work in and through your life.

The Counseling and Follow-Up Department
Billy Graham Evangelistic Association

All this is from God, who reconciled us to himself through Christ and gave us the ministry of reconciliation. . . . We are therefore Christ's ambassadors, as though God were making his appeal through us.

2 Corinthians 5:18, 20

Table of **C**ontents

General Introduction

Welcome to the Christian Life and Witness Course. You are joining thousands of others who through the years have attended a similar course in preparation for Christian service. Before the course begins it will be helpful to answer a few basic questions.

Who is the Christian Life and Witness Course for?

It is for every Christian who wants to know Jesus Christ better and wants to share Him with others. When you became a Christian, He gave you new life by the power of His Spirit in you. **It is the knowing and sharing of this new life that this course is designed to strengthen.** All followers of Jesus Christ can benefit from sharing together in this way.

Why is this course necessary?

It is always a good thing for Christians to have this type of course for preparation and training. **In the Christian life there are always new lessons to learn.** For those who are participating in the upcoming evangelistic event it is of special importance. This course will equip each of us to effectively share our faith. In addition, anyone who desires to be used as a counselor must attend the course.

How can I get the best from the course?

We realize that in a few short lessons it isn't possible to help every person become a mature, fully equipped worker. Therefore, the course objective is to give each participant a solid foundation for faith and some good, practical, basic principles upon which to build an effective Christian life and witness. **Here are a few suggestions to make the learning experience more effective:**

First—Come prepared to take notes. Each week the presentation will be different, and the subject matter will be presented in such a way that note taking should be easy. Many Scripture references will be given, and these should be useful later.

Second—Be faithful in completing your homework each week. This will involve a short Bible study, a project related to the lesson, and new Bible verses to memorize. According to educators, you forget a large percentage of what you hear. Therefore, if you are content to only listen to the lecture and not complete the home assignments, you may get very little of lasting value from the course.

Third—Think of how you might apply each lesson to your own life, and then pass on to others the truths, principles, suggestions or materials which you receive. In this way, you will learn to make practical use of them in your life first and then to invest your life in others.

Purpose of the Christian Life and Witness Course . . .

•**WALK**—The apostle Paul wrote about a daily relationship: *"So then, just as you received Christ Jesus as Lord, continue to live in him."* **Colossians 2:6**

•**WITNESS**—The apostle Peter gives us insight into evangelism: *"But in your hearts set apart Christ as Lord. Always be prepared to give an answer to everyone who asks you to give the reason for the hope that you have. But do this with gentleness and respect."* **1 Peter 3:15**

•**WORKERS**—Jesus told us how to pray: *"The harvest is plentiful, but the workers are few. Ask the Lord of the harvest, therefore, to send out workers into his harvest field."* **Luke 10:2**

•**FOLLOW-UP**—Paul helps us to understand the goal of our ministry: *"We proclaim him, admonishing and teaching everyone with all wisdom, so that we may present everyone perfect in Christ."* **Colossians 1:28**

•**INVESTMENT**—What we learn must be shared with others: *"And the things you have heard me say in the presence of many witnesses entrust to reliable men who will also be qualified to teach others."* **2 Timothy 2:2**

•**REVIVAL**—What we pray and long for: *"When I shut up the heavens so that there is no rain, or command locusts to devour the land or send a plague among my people, if my people, who are called by my name, will humble themselves and pray and seek my face and turn from their wicked ways, then will I hear from heaven and will forgive their sin and will heal their land."* **2 Chronicles 7:13–14**

<u>Notes</u>

LESSON ONE
The Effective Christian Life

Every Christian is responsible to live a life that glorifies God (**1 Corinthians 10:31**) and to be a true ambassador (**2 Corinthians 5:20**) for Him. Most Christians want to be used of God. For them it is not enough just to know they are on the Christian pathway, they want to be faithful and effective. The question is, **"How? Where do we start? What is involved?"**

In this class we will explore some of the key principles to effective Christian service. Perhaps the first answer can be found by looking at the life of Philip, who introduced the Ethiopian official to Jesus Christ in **Acts 8:26–38.** In this passage we can see five important principles:

First, God SOVEREIGNLY worked out all the details involved in Philip's effective witness to the Ethiopian. He will do the same for you.

Second, Philip's LIFE witnessed to Jesus Christ. He was chosen as a worker in the early church because of his character (**Acts 6:3–5**). A good life not only glorifies God but is a powerful witness to the world. Our lives should demonstrate that we know Him.

Third, we find the HOLY SPIRIT vitally involved in Philip's life and ministry. "The Spirit told Philip, 'Go to that chariot and stay near it'" (**Acts 8:29**). The Holy Spirit is the One who makes our lives attractive (**Galatians 5:22–23**). He is our Teacher and Guide. He gives us boldness and courage to witness. Our responsibility is to be yielded fully to all the wonderful resources of the Holy Spirit. Philip was led to someone already prepared.

Fourth, you will note the important part the SCRIPTURES play in telling another person about Jesus Christ. The Ethiopian was reading Isaiah 53 and asked Philip to explain the passage. Philip took the same passage, which deals prophetically with the crucifixion, and "told him the good news about Jesus" (**Acts 8:35**). Philip knew the Scriptures and was prepared to explain the good news of the Gospel. If we are going to be effective Christians, we too must gain a working knowledge of the Scriptures to help others.

Fifth, the Bible is a record of God working mightily in and through the lives of ordinary people. Our responsibility is to step out in FAITH and trust God to use us.

 Do you want to be used by God?

Grasping God's Word—What to Say

To be effective in God's work you must allow God's Word to fill your mind so you will know what to say, and to change your life so that you become someone He can use.

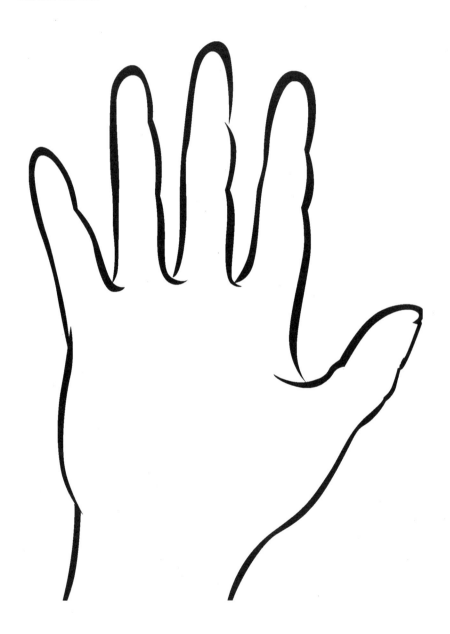

Romans 10:17—"Consequently, faith comes from hearing the message, and the message is heard through the word of Christ."

Deuteronomy 17:19—"It is to be with him, and he is to read it all the days of his life so that he may learn to revere the LORD his God and follow carefully all the words of this law and these decrees."

Proverbs 2:1–6—"My son, if you accept my words and store up my commands within you, turning your ear to wisdom and applying your heart to understanding, and if you call out for insight and cry aloud for understanding, and if you look for it as for silver and search for it as for hidden treasure, then you will understand the fear of the LORD and find the knowledge of God. For the LORD gives wisdom, and from his mouth come knowledge and understanding."

Psalm 119:9–11—"How can a young man keep his way pure? By living according to your word. I seek you with all my heart; do not let me stray from your commands. I have hidden your word in my heart that I might not sin against you."

Joshua 1:8—"Do not let this Book of the Law depart from your mouth; meditate on it day and night, so that you may be careful to do everything written in it. Then you will be prosperous and successful."

Grasping God's Hand—Power to Say It

No one can be an effective witness unless Christ is at work in them. He gives you the power and ability to speak of His continuing work in you.

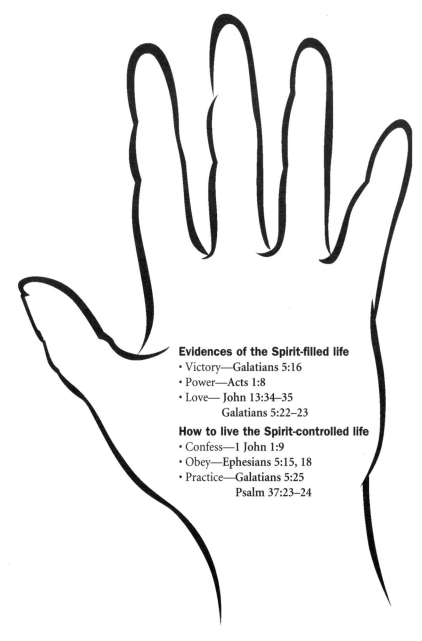

Evidences of the Spirit-filled life
- Victory—Galatians 5:16
- Power—Acts 1:8
- Love— John 13:34–35
    Galatians 5:22–23

How to live the Spirit-controlled life
- Confess—1 John 1:9
- Obey—Ephesians 5:15, 18
- Practice—Galatians 5:25
    Psalm 37:23–24

Jeremiah 1:6–9— " 'Ah, Sovereign LORD,' I said, 'I do not know how to speak; I am only a child.' But the LORD said to me, 'Do not say, "I am only a child." You must go to everyone I send you to and say whatever I command you. Do not be afraid of them, for I am with you and will rescue you,' declares the LORD. Then the LORD reached out his hand and touched my mouth and said to me, 'Now, I have put my words in your mouth.' "

Philippians 2:13— "For it is God who works in you to will and to act according to his good purpose."

Ephesians 5:15, 18— "Be very careful, then, how you live—not as unwise but as wise. . . . Do not get drunk on wine, which leads to debauchery. Instead, be filled with the Spirit."

Ephesians 6:17— "Take the helmet of salvation and the sword of the Spirit, which is the word of God."

Hebrews 11:1, 6— "Now faith is being sure of what we hope for and certain of what we do not see. . . . And without faith it is impossible to please God, because anyone who comes to him must believe that he exists and that he rewards those who earnestly seek him."

Legalism or Love

Legalism, or living by the letter of the law, is the cause of much division and contention in the church and in families. Our selfish attitudes can drive people away from us and the Lord. Only a gracious, loving attitude can bring unity, healing and forgiveness. The Holy Spirit is the source of God's love, and He dwells in each believer.

". . . the letter kills, but the Spirit gives life." **2 Corinthians 3:6**

Two _____

1. _____

2. _____

Four D's _____

1. _____

2. _____

3. _____

4. _____

Two _____

1. Don't _____

2. Don't _____

God's _____

Romans 5:5	Love's _____
1 Peter 4:8	Love _____
Colossians 3:12–14	Love _____

TAKE TIME AT HOME—Lesson One

Each week the lessons learned in the Christian Life and Witness Class should be practical. Someone once said, "The Bible was not written to increase our knowledge, but to make us more like Jesus Christ." Therefore, take time each week to review the lesson with your Bible and consider how you might apply what you learned.

HOME WORK	• Complete "The Effective Christian Life" Bible study. • Complete "The Effective Christian Life" project. • Memorize **Romans 3:23** and **Romans 6:23**. The verses and helpful suggestions on how to memorize are at the back of the book.

The Effective Christian Life—Bible Study

Please read the following questions carefully. Then open your Bible to the suggested passage. Study the passage and answer each question *briefly in your own words*.

Confidence in God's Sovereignty

The word *confidence* is taken from two words meaning "with faith." In other words, we put our confidence in God when we by faith trust Him to meet our needs and to use us in His service. It is thrilling to see how God uses individuals even though they are inadequate.

1. Your concept of God affects everything you do. Who is God and what is your responsibility to Him?

   _____

2. In which areas do the following verses encourage you to have confidence in God?

   Exodus 4:10–12 _____

   _____

   _____

   Judges 6:15–16 _____

   _____

   _____

   Jeremiah 1:6–9 _____

   _____

   _____

   Isaiah 41:10 _____

1 Corinthians 1:26–29 _____

_____

Philippians 4:13 _____

_____

Using God's Resources

3. Review the "Grasping God's Word" illustration on page 6. What lesson can you learn from this illustration?

_____

_____

4. Rewrite **Joshua 1:8** in your own words.

_____

_____

_____

5. Read **Acts 8:26–38** and review the "Grasping God's Hand" illustration on page 8 and answer the following questions.

a. How can you experience more of God's power?

_____

_____

_____

b. What is the secret of walking in the Spirit (being filled with the Spirit)?

_____

_____

_____

c. Why is it important to be filled with the Spirit (controlled by the Spirit)?

_____

_____

_____

The Effective Christian Life—Project

Love, the fruit of the Spirit, is clearly defined in the following passage. The effectiveness of our witness for Christ will be greatly determined by our love for others.

"Love is patient, love is kind. It does not envy, it does not boast, it is not proud. It is not rude, it is not self-seeking, it is not easily angered, it keeps no record of wrongs. Love does not delight in evil but rejoices with the truth. It always protects, always trusts, always hopes, always perseveres." **1 Corinthians 13:4–7**

1. Underline the different *aspects of love* found in the above passage and list them below.

Aspects of Love

_____   _____

_____   _____

_____   _____

_____   _____

2. Meditate on the various aspects of love and list areas of your life where you are weak or fall short in your relationships with others.

Areas Where I Fall Short

_____

_____

_____

_____

3. Write down what you can do to show more love to others.

Steps I Can Take Today

_____

_____

_____

_____

<u>Notes</u>

LESSON TWO
The Victorious Christian Life

 Why is it that some believers grow in Christ to become mature, well-balanced, fruitful Christians, while others spend most of their lives defeated, frustrated and unproductive?

The purpose of this lesson is to help us answer that question by examining two areas of our lives that can divert us from the plan and purposes of God. **First,** we look at adversity and **second,** we examine the reality of our sinful nature.

God's Word clearly speaks of a plan and purpose for our lives. We can enjoy a rich and abundant life if we walk obediently along God's Pathway. However, this does not mean that we will never encounter difficulties or experience adversity. Jesus told His followers that in this life they would have trouble **(John 16:33).**

To walk consistently along God's Pathway to victorious living, we also need to recognize that every believer has two natures. The **new nature** (Christ dwelling in us by His Spirit) desires to live obediently along God's Pathway . . . but the **old nature** (the flesh) pulls us in another direction, away from God.

Walking along God's Pathway does not come about by coincidence or accident. God is merciful and compassionate. He has made a provision for disobedient and wayward Christians to return to His Pathway if we are willing to admit our need and confess our sins. God will put us back on the Pathway to peace, joy and fullness of life.

This life takes dedication and surrender to Jesus Christ as Lord of our lives. The psalmist wrote:

> "Show me your ways, O LORD, teach me your paths; guide me in your truth and teach me, for you are God my Savior, and my hope is in you all day long." **Psalm 25:4–5**

Further, we are strengthened and encouraged each day by spending time alone with God. A daily "quiet time" spent in God's Word and prayer provides direction for our lives.

Adversity Builds Character

Every Christian will suffer adversity from time to time. In fact, the most godly people sometimes seem to suffer the greatest trials and afflictions. **Paul** had a physical infirmity (**2 Corinthians 12:7–10**). He also suffered from beatings, imprisonment, shipwreck, robbers and other dangers (**2 Corinthians 11:23–27**). **Job** lost his family, all his possessions, and was afflicted with terrible sores from head to foot. Yet he was a good man who hated evil (**Job 1:8, 22**). **Stephen** gave his life for the faith (**Acts 7:59–60**).

Adversities and afflictions *can be* a form of discipline that God uses in our lives when we need correction (**Psalm 119:67, 71, 75; Hebrews 12:6–10; 1 Corinthians 11:31–32**). *Normally,* adversities are a part of life to help in our Christian growth. They are meant to help remove some of the impurities from our lives and to deepen and develop our faith.

> "Remove the dross from the silver, and out comes material for the silversmith." **Proverbs 25:4**

Adversities can be stepping-stones to greater character and usefulness. But, too often, if we view them incorrectly, the trials of life will **discourage** and **depress** us. They can make us **bitter** instead of **better** and thus become a "stumbling block" instead of a "stepping-stone."

? What is your attitude toward adversity?

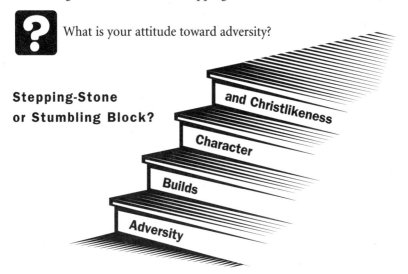

Stepping-Stone or Stumbling Block?

and Christlikeness

Character

Builds

Adversity

"Consider it pure **joy**, my brothers, whenever you face trials . . ." **James 1:2–4**
"We also **rejoice** in our sufferings . . ." **Romans 5:3–5**
"God works for the **good** of those who love him . . ." **Romans 8:28–29**
" . . . give **thanks** in all circumstances." **1 Thessalonians 5:16–18**

God's Pathway

When we receive Jesus Christ into our lives, all the promises of God are available to us. We experience these promises in our lives when we live as God directs. Since we do not always live perfectly, God has provided help to walk along His Pathway and to recover when we falter.

1. God's Promise: Fulfillment and Joy

> "Trust in the LORD with all your heart and lean not on your own understanding; in all your ways acknowledge him, and he will make your paths straight." **Proverbs 3:5–6**

There is a path that leads to fulfillment and meaning in life. The Bible is filled with promises for those who walk along God's Pathway. The Scriptures below contain just a few of these promises.

God's Way

"Walking in the Spirit"
"Walking in the light"
"Walking in truth"

RESULTS OF WALKING GOD'S PATHWAY

Victory and Fruitfulness
Galatians 5:16, 22–23

Cleansing and Fellowship
1 John 1:7–9

Companionship and Love
John 14:21
3 John 4

FULFILLMENT: "You have made known to me the path of life; you will fill me with joy in your presence, with eternal pleasures at your right hand." **Psalm 16:11**

SATISFACTION: "For he satisfies the thirsty and fills the hungry with good things." **Psalm 107:9**

PEACE: "You will keep in perfect peace him whose mind is steadfast, because he trusts in you." **Isaiah 26:3**

 Since God in His Word promises fulfillment and joy, why are many Christians today experiencing frustration, emptiness of life and unhappiness?

2. Our Problem: Sinful, Selfish Desires

When a Christian is diverted by adversity or sin from God's path, he or she will experience frustration, guilt, unhappiness and defeat. The Scriptures below show the problems which, if not dealt with, will pull an individual far away from God.

WALKING IN THE SPIRIT—God's Way
PEACE
JOY
FULLNESS OF LIFE

Our Way
Frustration
Guilt
Unhappiness
Defeat

SINFUL SELF: "I know that nothing good lives in me, that is, in my sinful nature. For I have the desire to do what is good, but I cannot carry it out." **Romans 7:18**

INNER CORRUPTION: "For from within, out of men's hearts, come evil thoughts, sexual immorality, theft, murder, adultery, greed, malice, deceit, lewdness, envy, slander, arrogance and folly." **Mark 7:21–22**

EVIL DESIRES: "When tempted, no one should say, 'God is tempting me.' For God cannot be tempted by evil, nor does he tempt anyone; but each one is tempted when, by his own evil desire, he is dragged away and enticed. Then, after desire has conceived, it gives birth to sin; and sin, when it is full-grown, gives birth to death." **James 1:13–15**

What selfish desire or sin has drawn you away from God, and what must you do to return to God's Pathway?

3. God's Provision: Forgiveness and Restoration

Although it is possible for us to stray from God's Pathway, God has wonderfully provided a way whereby the sidetracked Christian can get back onto God's Pathway and be restored to fellowship with Christ.

WALKING IN THE SPIRIT—God's Way

PEACE
JOY
FULLNESS OF LIFE

Our Way
Frustration
Guilt
Unhappiness
Defeat

STEP ONE   CONFESS. *Confess* means to "agree with God."

Confession: "If we confess our sins, he is faithful and just and will forgive us our sins and purify us from all unrighteousness." **1 John 1:9**

As we confess our sins to God, it is important to be specific and personal. If you have wronged someone, after making things right with God, make amends with the one you have wronged.

STEP TWO   FORSAKE YOUR SIN. Turn back to God's way made possible by the death of Christ on the cross and by His grace walk in obedience, strengthened by the Holy Spirit.

Forsake: "He who conceals his sins does not prosper, but whoever confesses and renounces them finds mercy." **Proverbs 28:13**

STEP THREE   ACCEPT GOD'S FORGIVENESS. The forgiveness of God is complete, perfect and forever!

Accept: "Then I acknowledged my sin to you and did not cover up my iniquity. I said, 'I will confess my transgressions to the LORD'—and you forgave the guilt of my sin." **Psalm 32:5**

Now that you have confessed and forsaken your waywardness, what must you do to maintain a steady walk along God's Pathway?

4. Our Practice: Dedication and Surrender

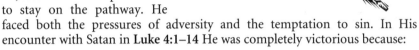

Having been restored to God's Pathway through God's love and forgiveness, we need to know how to avoid trouble again.

Jesus is our example of how to stay on the pathway. He faced both the pressures of adversity and the temptation to sin. In His encounter with Satan in **Luke 4:1–14** He was completely victorious because:

• He was filled and empowered with the Holy Spirit (v. 1).
• He was equipped with the Scriptures (v. 4).
• He had His mind set on the fulfillment of God's plan for Him.

To remain on God's Pathway we need:

A. A Set Mind

One of the secrets of all spiritual progress is a disciplined mind.

"But Daniel resolved not to defile himself."

Daniel 1:8

"Set your minds on things above, not on earthly things."

Colossians 3:2

Be careful this week about what you allow your thoughts to dwell on. Your predominant thought will give you immediate action:

SOW	REAP
a thought	an act
an act	a habit
a habit	a character
a character	a destiny

B. A Chosen Path

Make up your mind that you will not listen to any alternatives to God's pathway for you.

"I have chosen the way of truth; I have set my heart on your laws."

Psalm 119:30

C. A Daily Walk

The most practical way of keeping on God's Pathway, and developing a relationship with Jesus Christ that is fresh and radiant, is the daily "quiet time!"

Project:
For the next week start each day with **10 minutes** with the Lord. An outline for this time could be:

Take **five minutes** to review the Scriptures used in God's Pathway, pages 17–20.

Take the next **five minutes** and make each verse a personal prayer. Ask God to make these truths a part of your life. Then thank Him for His faithfulness and goodness toward you.

D. Right Priorities

When Jesus Christ is at the center of our lives, He provides the direction, wisdom, strength and the peace and joy. When we faithfully meet Him in Bible study and prayer, our priorities are rearranged and our life is lived in balance.

- **THE HUB—JESUS CHRIST**
  Galatians 2:20
- **PRAYER**
  Matthew 7:7
- **WORD**
  2 Timothy 3:15–17
- **WORSHIP**
  Hebrews 10:24–25
- **WITNESS**
  Matthew 4:19

A Set Mind, a Chosen Path, a Daily Walk and Right Priorities lead to a transformed life!

"Do not conform any longer to the pattern of this world, but be transformed by the renewing of your mind. Then you will be able to test and approve what God's will is—his good, pleasing and perfect will." **Romans 12:2**

TAKE TIME AT HOME
Lesson Two

HOME WORK
- Complete "The Victorious Christian Life" Bible study.
- Complete the "Quiet Time" project ("A Daily Walk," page 21).
- Memorize **Romans 5:8** and **Ephesians 2:8–9.**

The Victorious Christian Life—Bible Study

Review the God's Pathway illustration on pages 17–20 and answer the following questions:

1. Review the Scriptures on page 16—Adversity Builds Character. How can adversity be useful in our Christian growth?

   _____

   _____

   _____

2. List some of the rewards of Walking God's Pathway, page 17.

   _____

   _____

   _____

3. Review the Scriptures and diagram on page 18 and describe the *problem.*

   _____

   _____

   _____

4. Review the Scriptures and diagram on page 19 and explain God's *provision.*

   _____

   _____

   _____

5. According to Luke 4:1–14, how can you consistently walk on God's Pathway?

_____

_____

_____

6. What does the wheel diagram illustrate? Page 21.

_____

_____

_____

7. Which spoke in the wheel illustration on page 21 is weakest in your life? List practical ways to strengthen it.

_____

_____

_____

8. According to Luke 6:46 and John 14:21, how can you best demonstrate that Jesus Christ is your Lord and that you love Him?

_____

_____

_____

<u>Notes</u>

LESSON THREE
The Christian's Witness

So far in the course we have been stressing personal preparation for a close walk with God. Before we begin our third lesson on a Christian's witness, let's ask some important questions:

 Do you have faith in the power and sovereignty of God?

 Do you believe that God can use you in spite of your own weakness and inadequacy?

 Do you believe that the Holy Spirit will guide you, make you courageous, help you in your work, and also work effectively in the lives of those to whom you will speak?

 Do you believe that "the word of God is living and active. Sharper than any double-edged sword, it penetrates even to dividing soul and spirit, joints and marrow; it judges the thoughts and attitudes of the heart"? (**Hebrews 4:12**).

 Do you believe that the Gospel of Christ is the "power of God for the salvation of everyone who believes"? (**Romans 1:16**).

Did you answer the above questions positively? If yes, then witnessing for Jesus Christ is something you can do. Remember, "the battle is not yours, but God's" (**2 Chronicles 20:15**). If we follow the example of the apostle Peter, God will use us in the lives of others to introduce them to the Good News of the Gospel.

> "But in your hearts set apart Christ as Lord. Always be prepared to give an answer to everyone who asks you to give the reason for the hope that you have. But do this with gentleness and respect."
>
> **1 Peter 3:15**

Following are some practical things about your witness to keep in mind:

First—*Your own life is a great part of your witness.* The apostle Paul wrote, "for it is God who works in you" (**Philippians 2:13**). If God is at work, then you have something good to share. You don't need to be perfect before God can use you, but your life should reflect the Lord Jesus Christ. Remember, the Holy Spirit works more effectively through a clean life (**2 Corinthians 4:2**).

Second—*Earn the right to be heard by sincerely listening to others.* People are hurting today and searching for answers as never before. Perhaps their greatest need is to find someone who cares. Everybody needs a friend. Jesus was called "a friend of sinners." People from every walk of life knew that Jesus sincerely cared for them. Very few people have the "gift" of evangelism—but every Christian can be a friend. We can all be involved in building bridges of friendship that may lead to natural opportunities to share the "good news" about Jesus Christ. Start by:
- Winning the confidence of people by sharing genuine interest.
- Letting them share concerns, opinions and hurts.
- Not feeling compelled to always do the talking! Listen!

It may mean that you must get more deeply involved in someone's life. But in the long run you will develop trust and have a more sympathetic individual with whom you can discuss the claims of Jesus Christ.

Third—*You are presenting the Person of Jesus Christ.* Jesus is alive! It is not a formula, outline or theological system that you have a relationship with—it is the Person of Jesus as Lord and Savior. The Scriptures you have learned and memorized should give you confidence. However, do not make the mistake of thinking that you must always begin with your Bible, turning from passage to passage. Be sensitive to the individual and to the Lord's prompting and use the Scriptures wisely.

Fourth—*Stress the love of God.* We must admit that we are sinners and we all need the Savior for cleansing and forgiveness. But this does not mean we start there! It is best to present the love of God before the judgment of God.

Fifth—*Keep it simple.* Don't make the mistake of thinking that you have to "prove" the Gospel—or create an intellectual argument to impress people. The apostle Paul stayed with the simplicity of the Gospel, and God blessed His Word tremendously. "When I came to you, brothers, I did not come with eloquence or superior wisdom as I proclaimed to you the testimony about God. For I resolved to know nothing while I was with you except Jesus Christ and him crucified" (**1 Corinthians 2:1–2**).

THE BRIDGE TO LIFE ILLUSTRATION

Share Facts   **Invite**   **Pray**   **Confirm**

God's Plan—

Our Problem—

God's Remedy—

Our Response—

Remember:
- Share the facts of the Gospel
- Illustrate it from your own experience
- Give opportunity for questions and discussion
- Invite a response and have prayer
- Give assurance when necessary

Instructions For Using "My Commitment"

1. Introduce yourself to the inquirer and get the person's name so you can use it in conversation.

2. Ask the question: *"Have you come forward to personally accept Jesus Christ as your Lord and Savior?"*
   - If "Yes" review page 6, *"How to Receive Christ,"* to make sure the inquirer fully understands the commitment.
   - If the inquirer wants to personally accept Jesus Christ as their Lord and Savior, encourage them to pray the prayer at the bottom of page 6.
   - Following the prayer, turn to page 2, *"Salvation."*
   - Explain step-by-step the short lesson on the page.
   - Hold the folder in such a way that the inquirer can follow along.
   - When you come to a question, be patient and give the inquirer time to answer. Let him or her write in the answers.
   - The goal is to make sure the commitment is confirmed by Scripture.
   - Give the "My Commitment" folder to the inquirer when finished. Suggest that he or she review the Scriptures later, especially when tempted to doubt or get discouraged.

3. If the inquirer answers *"No"* to the question *"Have you come forward to personally accept Jesus Christ as your Lord and Savior?"* Have the individual examine the other statements.

4. If the inquirer checks "I am not sure. I need assurance," do the following:
   - Review *"How to Receive Christ"* on page 6. This is to ensure that the inquirer has a genuine understanding of the Gospel.
   - If the inquirer wants to personally accept Jesus Christ as their Lord and Savior, encourage them to pray the prayer at the bottom of page 6.
   - If they already know Christ personally, turn to page 3 and the lesson *"How to Be Sure You Have Eternal Life."* Many people lack assurance because:
     —They have not really understood the Gospel.
     —They have trusted in their feelings instead of what Jesus did on the cross for them.
     —They feel that some area of failure has separated them from God.
   - Explain step-by-step the short lesson on assurance on page 3. The goal of this lesson is to make sure the commitment is confirmed by Scripture.

5. **If the inquirer checks "I have failed to follow Christ and want to rededicate my life to Him" do the following:**
   - Review *"How to Receive Christ"* on page 6. This is to ensure that the inquirer has a genuine understanding of the Gospel.
   - If the inquirer wants to personally accept Jesus Christ as their Lord and Savior, encourage them to pray the prayer at the bottom of page 6.
   - If they already know Christ personally, turn to page 4 and the lesson *"How to Come Back to Christ."* Help the inquirer see the need to confess his or her failures and be restored.
   - Explain step-by-step the short lesson on rededication. The goal of this lesson is to make sure their recommitment is confirmed by Scripture.

6. **If the inquirer checks "I want to demonstrate my faith" do the following:**
   - Review *"How to Receive Christ"* on page 6. This is to ensure that the inquirer has a genuine understanding of the Gospel.
   - If the inquirer wants to personally accept Jesus Christ as their Lord and Savior, encourage them to pray the prayer at the bottom of page 6.
   - If they already know Christ personally, encourage the inquirer and have prayer.
   - Give him or her the appropriate follow-up literature.

7. **If the inquirer checks "I want to talk about a special need I have" do the following:**
   - If it is about an understanding of the Gospel, review *"How to Receive Christ"* on page 6.
   - If the inquirer wants to personally accept Jesus Christ as their Lord and Savior, encourage them to pray the prayer at the bottom of page 6.
   - If they pray to receive Christ proceed to the lesson on page 2, *"Salvation."*
   - If they have a particular personal problem, seek help from a pastor.

8. **If the inquirer checks "I want to know more about what it means to receive Christ," do the following:**
   - Review *"How to Receive Christ"* on page 6.
   - If the inquirer wants to personally accept Jesus Christ as their Lord and Savior, encourage them to pray the prayer at the bottom of page 6.
   - After he or she prays to receive Christ proceed to the lesson on page 2, *"Salvation."*
   - If the inquirer *does not* receive Christ, turn to page 5 and review the steps *"For Further Help."*

9. As you close out the counseling session, be sure that you have:

- Answered question one of the Bible study *Beginning Your Christian Life*.
- Reviewed the memory verse cards inside *Beginning Your Christian Life*.
- Encouraged further reading in the gospel of John.
- Emphasized the importance of attending church and telling others about his or her faith in Christ.
- Closed with prayer. Always have prayer with each inquirer.
- Completed the Counselor Card, checked it carefully and kept the bottom copy for personal reference and handed the top copy to a card collector.
- Filled out the small "My Decision" card and given the inquirer your name, phone number, or an e-mail address for future help if appropriate.

If at any time in the conversation with the inquirer you are unsure about his or her commitment to Christ or understanding of the Gospel, the following questions may be helpful to clarify the person's spiritual condition:

- *"When did you receive Jesus Christ as your personal Lord and Savior?"* If you still have doubts, ask . . .
- *"If you were to die tonight, would you go to heaven?"* If you are still not sure, ask . . .
- *"If you were to stand before God and He were to say, 'Why should I accept you into my heaven?', what would you say?"*

TAKE TIME AT HOME
Lesson Three

HOME WORK
- Complete "The Christian's Witness" Bible study.
- Complete "The Christian's Witness" project.
- Memorize **Revelation 3:20** and **John 1:12**.

The Christian's Witness—Bible Study

Review the *Steps to Peace with God* booklet and the *Bridge to Life* illustration on page 27 and answer the following questions.

1. What is the Gospel? **1 Corinthians 15:1–4**

_____

_____

_____

2. What power does the Gospel possess? **Romans 1:16**

_____

_____

_____

3. What is our basic spiritual PROBLEM? Why do we need salvation? **Romans 3:23; 6:23**

_____

_____

_____

4. According to **Romans 5:8** and **Ephesians 2:8–9**, what was God's REMEDY for our problem? What did Jesus Christ do for sinners?

_____

_____

_____

5. How must we RESPOND? How does a person become a Christian—a child of God? **Acts 3:19; John 1:12**

_____

_____

_____

6. According to **John 3:1–16** what does it mean to be "born again"?

_____

_____

_____

7. In His witness to the woman of Samaria and to Nicodemus, Jesus varied His approach. How was it different? **John 3:1–8; John 4:1–15**

_____

_____

_____

The Christian's Witness—Project

1. Pray for one person this week with whom you might share *Steps to Peace with God.*

   Make an appointment and tell the person you want to talk about something you are learning in the **Christian Life and Witness Classes.**

   Before you do that, appeal to his or her intellect by saying, "I would like to get your reaction to this booklet."

   Pray that God will give you the words to say and that He would open his or her eyes.

2. Sharing your **testimony,** a personal story of your relationship with Jesus Christ, can be very effective in witnessing. Write out the following:

   • Describe briefly your life before you met Jesus Christ as Lord and Savior.

   _____

   _____

   _____

   _____

   • What were the circumstances surrounding your commitment to Jesus Christ?

   _____

   _____

   _____

   _____

   • Briefly describe your life after receiving Jesus Christ.

   _____

   _____

   _____

   _____

<u>Notes</u>

LESSON FOUR
Follow-Up and the Care of New Christians

Today we need to see the importance of what we do before we share the Gospel and what we do after someone has received Christ.

Operation Andrew is a friendship evangelism ministry based on **John 1:41–42:** *"The first thing Andrew did was to find his brother Simon and tell him, 'We have found the Messiah' (that is, the Christ). And he brought him to Jesus."*

OPERATION ANDREW
is five simple steps

1 **LOOK AROUND**—Your mission field is right where you live, work or go to school. List names of individuals you know who need Jesus Christ. Pray for them regularly.

2 **LOOK UP**—God changes people through prayer. Pray each day for the people on your list, asking God to give you opportunities to talk about His love with them.

3 **LOOK OUT**—Find ways to cultivate friendships with the people on your list. Earn their confidence; spend time with them. Friendships open the way to talk about Christ.

4 **LOOK FORWARD**—Talk with each person on your list about attending a special evangelistic event with you. Choose a specific date and invite them.

5 **LOOK AFTER**—Those who respond to Christ or show interest in the Gospel need your encouragement. Continue to pray for those who respond to the Gospel and those who do not.

Through the personal ministry of Operation Andrew and the faithful presentation of the Gospel, many people will find new life in Christ. As we prepare to evangelize, several important questions remain:

What will happen to those who respond to the preaching of the Gospel?

Will they remain faithful to their commitment?

Will they take their place in the church?

Will they grow to become effective witnesses for Christ?

Jesus frequently spoke of sharing the Gospel as being like a farmer sowing seed. For example, in the parable of the sower in **Mark 4,** we learn that not everyone who hears the Good News will grow and mature; there are some disappointing results. However, we can also learn from this parable that many do respond and will grow and mature spiritually. Indeed, years of evangelistic experience has proven this over and over again.

As we think about a commitment to Christ, the initial decision to receive Christ is just the beginning. Continued spiritual growth and effectiveness will largely be determined by the amount of spiritual care and prayer given on their behalf. In fact, most of the books of the New Testament were letters of concern for young believers written by the apostle Paul. In a real sense they were "follow-up" letters to encourage the spiritual growth of churches and individuals.

The apostle Paul was an energetic pacesetter in the area of spiritual pediatrics—that's the caring for new believers. Consider the following verses from Paul's letters and from Acts:

"We were not looking for praise from men, not from you or anyone else. As apostles of Christ we could have been a burden to you, but we were gentle among you, like a mother caring for her little children. We loved you so much that we were delighted to share with you not only the gospel of God but our lives as well, because you had become so dear to us."

1 Thessalonians 2:6–8

"Night and day we pray most earnestly that we may see you again and supply what is lacking in your faith."

1 Thessalonians 3:10

"We sent Timothy, who is our brother and God's fellow worker in spreading the gospel of Christ, to strengthen and encourage you in your faith."

1 Thessalonians 3:2

"The reason I wrote you was to see if you would stand the test and be obedient in everything."

2 Corinthians 2:9

"Some time later Paul said to Barnabas, 'Let us go back and visit the brothers in all the towns where we preached the word of the Lord and see how they are doing.'"

Acts 15:36

Paul's methods and strategy were effective and fruitful. These verses teach important strategies for our work.

STRATEGY 1 Paul gave himself—*1 Thessalonians 2:6–8*

Though it was very costly in every way—emotionally, financially, in time, in travel, in study, in writing, in criticism from others—Paul was "delighted" to give it all to see men and women come to faith in Christ and go on with Him. Often the greatest obstacle to evangelism is our unwillingness to give ourselves and become involved with other people.

STRATEGY 2 Paul prayed for them—*1 Thessalonians 3:10*

His prayer was earnest and persistent. Again and again in Paul's writing he tells the new believers how frequently he prayed. See also 1 Thessalonians 1:2–3; 2:13.

STRATEGY 3 Paul sent others—*1 Thessalonians 3:2*

When he couldn't do all he wanted to personally, he sent others he had trained to strengthen and encourage new believers.

STRATEGY 4 Paul wrote letters—*2 Corinthians 2:9*

All of Paul's writings in the New Testament are in the form of "follow-up" letters. Answering questions, encouraging, instructing, correcting.

STRATEGY 5 Paul returned—*Acts 15:36*

When he wrote to the Thessalonians, Paul asked them to pray with him that he would have opportunity to return. Frequently on his missionary journeys Paul stopped not only to preach the Gospel to those who had never heard, but to teach and encourage new Christians.

Paul's primary concern overall was for the growth and spiritual development of new Christians. **His goal was their maturity.**

"My dear children, for whom I am again in the pains of childbirth until Christ is formed in you, how I wish I could be with you now and change my tone, because I am perplexed about you!"

Galatians 4:19–20

"We proclaim him, admonishing and teaching everyone with all wisdom, so that we may present everyone perfect in Christ."

Colossians 1:28

The precedent is clearly set. New Christians do need care, and every effort must be made to provide it. That care should be provided by *someone*—and that someone is logically the person who prayed for, befriended, invited and brought the person to meet Jesus Christ. This is spiritual adoption—the "spiritual parent" needs to be available to offer help, counsel, encourage, guide in the Scripture, teach how to pray and help to provide for regular church attendance. The Holy Spirit and the Word of God do their work, and we must do ours.

DEFINITION: *Follow-up* is the process of giving continued attention to new Christians until they are at home in the local church, find out how they can serve, develop their full potential for Jesus Christ and help to build Christ's church.

Needs of a New Christian

1. 1 Peter 2:2 _____

2. 1 Peter 5:8 _____

3. Colossians 2:6–7 _____

Remember . . . new Christians need someone, not something!

". . . but we were gentle among you, like a mother caring for her little children."

1 Thessalonians 2:7

Counselor Follow-Up

A clear commitment to Jesus Christ is the first step to ensure effective follow-up. As a counselor for the upcoming evangelistic event, pray that the Holy Spirit will help you to meet the needs of the new believers.

The task of the counselor can be summarized as follows:

- To help the inquirer understand his or her relationship to Jesus Christ by using the "My Commitment" folder.
- To carefully go through the Bible study *Beginning Your Christian Life*. This study is designed to establish good priorities and a devotional habit and to begin spiritual growth.
- To record information about the inquirer on the counselor card so that he or she may be contacted by the local church.
- To begin the important work of follow-up during the first few days after the initial commitment.

Let's look at each area in greater detail:

First—To help the inquirer understand his or her relationship with Jesus Christ by using the "My Commitment" folder.
- The difference between counseling at an evangelistic event and personal witnessing is that in counseling the explanation of the Gospel and the call to commitment has been done by the evangelist. As a counselor you simply need to understand the step the inquirer has taken.
- Pray for the Holy Spirit to make you sensitive in this area.
- The inquirer may respond in any one of the five areas.
  —Acceptance of Christ
  —Assurance
  —Rededication
  —Special Needs
  —A desire to know more.
- Remember, sometimes people do not fully understand the Gospel. Therefore, in all cases take care to review *"How to Receive Christ"* on page 6 of the "My Commitment" folder.
- Pray with the inquirer if they want to personally accept Jesus Christ as Lord and Savior.
- Then proceed to follow the instructions on the cover of the "My Commitment" folder.

Second—Carefully go through the Bible study *Beginning Your Christian Life.*
- Review "How to Use This Booklet" in *Beginning Your Christian Life.*

- Find the gospel of John and encourage daily reading using the reading guide.
- Turn to the Bible memory verses. Encourage Scripture memory and review on a daily basis.
- Examine the four Bible studies on: "Knowing Christ," "Growing in Christ," "Obeying Christ," and "Witnessing for Christ."
- Turn to the first study, "Knowing Christ," and help the inquirer answer the first questions of the Bible study.
- After going through *Beginning Your Christian Life:*

Third—Record information about the inquirer on the counselor card so that he or she may be contacted by a local church.
- This is **very** important. All the follow-up work depends on complete and accurate information.
- Use a ballpoint pen. Soft tip and pencil will not work.
- Print neatly and carefully.
- Fill out **all** information. Take great care when filling out the inquirer address and church relationship.
- Examine the top copy to be turned in. Is it legible?
- Examine the bottom copy. Can you read it? This is the copy you retain.
- Tear both copies out of the booklet—counselor keeps the bottom copy.
- The top copy is handed to a card collector or supervisor before leaving the counseling area.

Fourth—Begin the important work of follow-up during the first few days after the initial commitment.
- Before leaving the inquirer, fill out the "My Decision" card with the date of commitment and have the inquirer sign it. If appropriate, fill out the back so the inquirer has your name, phone number and an e-mail address. This is to encourage future contact for assistance as needed.
- Within 48 hours each counselor is asked to PHONE/E-MAIL/WRITE or VISIT the inquirer(s) counseled.
- When you contact the inquirer by the appropriate method encourage:
    —Completion of the *Beginning Your Christian Life* Bible study.
    —Devotional reading and Scripture memory.
    —Church attendance.
    —Attendance at a Bible study.
    —Witness for Christ by telling others what Christ has done for him or her.
- And remember to pray for the inquirer daily. You may be the only Christian they know!

"Being confident of this, that he who began a good work in you will carry it on to completion until the day of Christ Jesus."   **Philippians 1:6**

Counselor's Sample of Follow-Up Letter

NOTE: This letter is provided only as a guideline for the letter you should write. Make your letter personal and helpful for the situation.

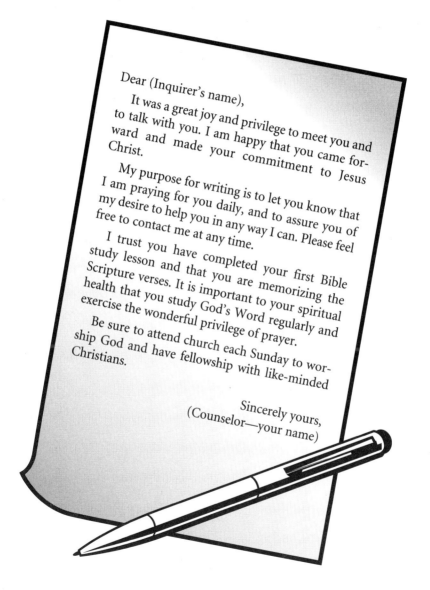

Dear (Inquirer's name),

It was a great joy and privilege to meet you and to talk with you. I am happy that you came forward and made your commitment to Jesus Christ.

My purpose for writing is to let you know that I am praying for you daily, and to assure you of my desire to help you in any way I can. Please feel free to contact me at any time.

I trust you have completed your first Bible study lesson and that you are memorizing the Scripture verses. It is important to your spiritual health that you study God's Word regularly and exercise the wonderful privilege of prayer.

Be sure to attend church each Sunday to worship God and have fellowship with like-minded Christians.

Sincerely yours,
(Counselor—your name)

<u>Notes</u>

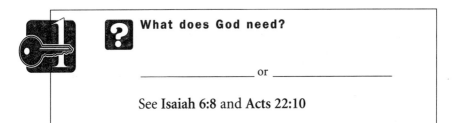

What does God need?

_____ or _____

See Isaiah 6:8 and Acts 22:10

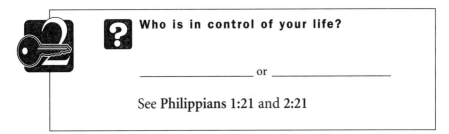

Who is in control of your life?

_____ or _____

See Philippians 1:21 and 2:21

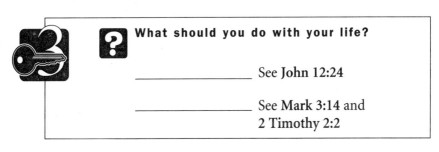

What should you do with your life?

_____ See John 12:24

_____ See Mark 3:14 and
2 Timothy 2:2

Start where you are . . . with what you have . . . and do your best. Remember, "it is God who works in you to will and to act according to his good purpose" (Philippians 2:13).

TAKE TIME AT HOME
Lesson Four

HOME WORK

• Complete the "Follow-Up and the Care of New Christians" Bible study.
• Review memory verses each day.
• Read *Beginning Your Christian Life* and do the Bible studies.
• Read "Procedures for Counseling" on pages 49–51.

Follow-Up and the Care of New Christians— Bible Study

1. The apostle Paul had a very effective ministry in Thessalonica. Briefly summarize what took place in 1 Thessalonians 1:2–10.

_____

_____

_____

2. According to 1 Thessalonians 2:7–8, what was the key to the apostle Paul's success in follow-up?

_____

_____

_____

3. Write out your own definition of *follow-up*.

_____

_____

_____

4. According to Mark 4:1–20, why is follow-up so important?

_____

_____

_____

The Lord Jesus, our master teacher, introduced a principle which all of us can practice. Though He ministered to the public, He often spent time with a few. Through this intimate contact, Jesus shared His life and challenged His disciples to spread the Gospel.

5. What are the main principles in the vital work of caring for new Christians that can be learned from:

Mark 3:14 _____

_____

Matthew 28:19–20 _____

_____

2 Timothy 2:2 _____

_____

6. How can you be a part of feeding, protecting and training Crusade inquirers? List two or three specific ways you can help:

• _____

• _____

• _____

APPENDIX

- **Procedures for Counseling**

- **Helpful Reminders**

- **Review**

- **Helps in Witnessing**

- **Objections and Excuses**

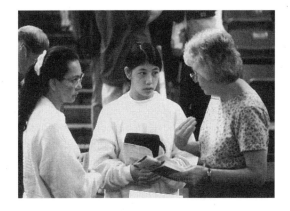

Procedures For Counseling

GENERAL INFORMATION

Preliminary Instructions

- Always bring your Bible or New Testament and a ballpoint pen.
- Be neat and clean in your personal appearance; something to sweeten the breath is recommended.
- Counselors should work with those of their own gender and general age group.

Counseling Materials

- *Beginning Your Christian Life* packets should be issued to each counselor.
- *Jesus is My Friend* should be issued for use with children 10 years of age and under. These packets are decidedly different from adult packets. Always make certain that you have the right packet.
- **Please return unused packets.** They are costly and **should not be carried away.** If you care to purchase additional materials, this can be done through Grason/World Wide Publications, P.O. Box 1240, Minneapolis, Minnesota 55440-1240. Call 800-487-0433, Fax 612-335-1398, or e-mail grasoncs@bgea.org.

THE INVITATION

Coming Forward

- The evangelist will invite inquirers to come forward and stand in front of the platform or other designated area.
- If you are seated with a group of counselors in an assigned area you will be directed by the supervisor in your section as to when you should follow an inquirer to the front of the platform.
- If someone near you of the same gender and approximate age responds, accompany that person to the front of the platform.
- The Follow-Up Card (the top copy) is detached and given to the supervisor or a "Collector."
- IT IS OF THE UTMOST IMPORTANCE THAT THE CARD BE FILLED OUT LEGIBLY AND COMPLETELY.
  - —Get complete and accurate information.
  - —Some 60% of the cards may need further research each night because information is lacking.

—Incomplete or inaccurate information delays follow-up.
• Go over the person's name and address to make sure you have it correctly.
—The name must be printed PLAINLY.
—The name should be printed in the same order as indicated on the card, i.e., Last Name, First Name, Middle Initial.

Counselor's Card

Miss
Mrs.
Ms.
Mr._____ Age _____
    (Last Name)   (First Name)   (Middle Initial)

—Be careful to indicate whether the inquirer is Mr., Mrs., Miss, or Ms.
—Be sure you get the address where the inquirer can be reached and include the street number and zip/post code.
• If the individual is reluctant to give age, or if it seems unwise to ask, write the approximate age.
• The telephone number and an e-mail address should be placed on the card for further follow-up.
• Mark only **one** of the decision squares.
• Inform the inquirer that we desire to send their name to a local pastor for church follow-up.
—Ask, "Do you attend a local church?"
—If yes, write how often and the church information, including church name, pastor's name, and **complete** church address.
—If the person was brought by a friend or church group and would like to be referred to that church, OR if the person has a preference for a particular church other than the one now attending, record this information under "Which church invited you?"
• Perhaps the biggest problem in follow-up is insufficient information about the church.
—Write down the full name and street number of the church.
—Fill in the city, state/province, and zip/post code.
—If you cannot get the pastor's full first name, try to get an initial.
• The information concerning the individual's occupation or school is useful in special follow-up.
• BE SURE THAT **YOUR NAME** IS **PRINTED** ON THE CARD.
• PLEASE NOTE: If the person **does not** desire to be referred to a church and **does not** want a pastor to visit

OR

If the person does not want to receive any follow-up material by mail

OR

If you have additional, *pertinent* information concerning the inquirer

THEN

Write "See Back" on the bottom of your Counselor Card.

Then write your comments on the back of the Follow-Up Card (top copy).

- The information on the Counselor's Card is confidential and must be treated as such.
- After completion of the Counselor's Card be sure to give your name, address, and phone number to the inquirer using the little card "My Decision" provided in the *Beginning Your Christian Life* booklet. Encourage the inquirer to contact you for help, or if further questions arise as appropriate.
- There will be a special counseling area for children age 10 and under. Certain counselors and supervisors, experienced in working with children, will be selected for this area. They will have additional instructions.
- Hand in only the "Follow-Up Card" (top copy) to the supervisor or collector.
   —Retain the back copy (Counselor's Card) for your record.
   —Be sure to write with sufficient pressure that the Counselor's Card (duplicate bottom copy) is legible.
   —If for some reason the bottom copy is not legible, please do what is necessary to make it legible and complete.

Notes

Helpful Reminders

- DO use your Bible (Psalm 19:7) . . . DON'T present your own ideas.
- DO use the Bible as a sword (Ephesians 6:17) . . . DON'T use it as a club (Ephesians 4:15).
- DO encourage response . . . DON'T force a decision.
- DO ask questions . . . DON'T take anything for granted.
- DO be a good listener . . . DON'T do all the talking (Proverbs 18:13).
- DO be polite . . . DON'T argue (2 Timothy 2:24).
- DO be positive and show what they gain through Christ . . . DON'T overemphasize the negative.
- DO be interested in them . . . DON'T pry into their affairs.
- DO be friendly . . . DON'T be familiar.
- DO be considerate . . . DON'T delay unnecessarily.
- DO speak as an equal and identify with the person . . . DON'T preach.
- DO be kind . . . DON'T run down another's faith or denomination.
- DO be brief and simple . . . DON'T try to give them a full Bible course.
- DO keep faith with the inquirer . . . DON'T betray their confidence.
- DO be pleasant, smile . . . DON'T scowl!

 Review

The following statements are based on the counseling procedures. They are either true or false. Read each statement carefully and circle the appropriate letter.

T	**F**	1. The top copy of the Counselor's Card is for the inquirer.
T	**F**	2. It is important to let the inquirer read the Scripture passages for themselves during the counseling.
T	**F**	3. The counseling packet for children differs from that for adults.
T	**F**	4. Counselors should never force a decision.
T	**F**	5. The name of only one inquirer should be written on the Counselor's Card.
T	**F**	6. In counseling, you should help those of your own gender.

T	F	7. Each inquirer should base assurance on the Word of God.
T	F	8. It is not necessary to return unused packets.
T	F	9. Certain counselors will be designated to counsel children 10 and under.
T	F	10. After the training course is over, counselors should lessen their Bible study, devotional life and witnessing.
T	F	11. It is important to help the inquirer start on the Bible study the night of the decision by letting them answer the first question.
T	F	12. It is important for you to contact each person you counsel within 48 hours by personal visit, letter, telephone or e-mail.
T	F	13. Only the name and address of the inquirer is needed on the Counselor's Card.

NOTE: Please keep this true-false test for your information.

Ministry Resources

The following books have proven effective in strengthening and encouraging Christians to live faithfully for Jesus Christ. Contact your local Christian bookstore to secure these and other excellent materials.

Personal Ministry

Christian Worker's Handbook, World Wide Publications, 800-487-0433

How to Give Away Your Faith, Paul Little, InterVarsity Press, 800-843-9487

Learning to Walk with God, Charles Riggs, World Wide Publications, 800-487-0433

Lifestyle Evangelism, Joe Aldrich, Multnomah Press, Lay Renewal Ministries 314-647-6717

The Master Plan of Evangelism, Robert E. Coleman, Baker Book House

Mere Christianity, C. S. Lewis, Macmillan

Out of the Saltshaker, Rebecca Pippert, InterVarsity Press, 800-843-9487

Overcoming Walls to Witnessing, Timothy Beougher, World Wide Publications, 800-487-0433

Peace with God, Billy Graham, Word, Inc., 800-487-0433

Scripture Memory

Memory Verse Packets, World Wide Publications, 800-487-0433

Scripture Memory Motivator, World Wide Publications, 800-487-0433

Topical Memory System, NavPress, 800-366-7788

Personal Devotions

Believer's Daily Renewal, Andrew Murray, Bethany House Publishers, 800-328-6109

The Believer's Secret of Intercession, Andrew Murray, Bethany House Publishers, 800-328-6109

Experiencing God, Henry T. Blackaby, Broadman & Holman, 800-251-3225

Joy and Strength, Mary Wilder Tileston, World Wide Publications, 800-487-0433

Making His Heart Glad, Marie Chapian, Bethany House Publishers, 800-328-6109

My Utmost for His Highest - revised, Oswald Chambers, Thomas Nelson Publishers, Barbour, 800-446-6240

The One Year Bible, Tyndale House Publishers

Quiet Time (An InterVarsity Guidebook for Daily Devotions), InterVarsity Press, 800-843-0487

Seven Minutes with God (How to Plan a Daily Quiet Time), NavPress, 800-366-7788

Streams in the Desert, Mrs. Charles Cowman, Zondervan Publishers, 800-727-1309

Thirty Discipleship Exercises, World Wide Publications, 800-487-0433

Unto the Hills, Billy Graham, Word, Inc., 800-487-0433

Prayer

Personal Prayer Journal, World Wide Publications, 800-487-0433

Prayer: The Great Adventure, David Jeremiah, Multnomah, Lay Renewal Ministries, 314-647-6717

Too Busy Not to Pray, Bill Hybels, InterVarsity Press, 800-843-9487

Bible Study

Growing Deep in the Christian Life, Chuck Swindoll, Zondervan Publishers, 800-727-1309

Christian Growth Series

All materials used in the Christian Life and Witness Course are available for church- and community-based ministry. They include the *Christian Life and Witness Course* book and a four-part video series and other related materials. For more information on these materials contact World Wide Publications at 800-487-0433, fax: 612-335-1398, or E-mail: grasoncs@bgea.org.

Helps in Witnessing

If you thoroughly examine the subjects and memorize the Scriptures, you will find frequent use of this material.

AFFLICTIONS

Are often providential ....Psalm 119:67, 71, 75

God will deliver ....Psalm 34:19

ANXIETY

Is relieved through prayer..Philippians 4:6–7

Remember . . . God cares for you......................................1 Peter 5:7

ASSURANCE

Eternal life promised .... John 3:16

You can be sure ....1 John 5:11–13

COMFORT

Jesus—the Good Shepherd ....Psalm 23

He will never forsake you...Hebrews 13:5–6

DISCOURAGEMENT

Don't give up ....Galatians 6:9

God will help and strengthen ....Isaiah 41:10

EMPTINESS

Christ can satisfy ....Psalm 107:8–9

He will fulfill your desires...Psalm 37:4–5

FORGIVENESS

Forgiveness and cleansing promised ....Psalm 32:5; 1 John 1:9

GUILT

No condemnation ....Romans 8:1

No sin too great..Isaiah 1:18

JUDGMENT

Everyone accountable...Romans 14:12; Hebrews 9:27

LONELINESS

His presence promised ....Hebrews 13:5–6

In His presence is joy ....Psalm 16:11

SUFFERING

Suffering has profit...Hebrews 12:6–11

It deepens the faith ....1 Peter 1:6–7

It's to be expected...1 Peter 2:19–23

God's grace is sufficient ....2 Corinthians 12:9–10

TEMPTATIONS

How to avoid them...Matthew 26:41

What causes failure...James 1:13–14

VICTORY

Is in Christ ....Philippians 4:13

Your inner resource ....1 John 4:4

Seek God's help..1 Corinthians 10:13

WORRY

God will provide..Philippians 4:19

Have faith in Him..Romans 4:20–21

Claim His promises ....1 John 5:14–15

Objections and Excuses

CLASS 1 Attendance—Please Print

Name _____ Age _____ Date _____

Street Address _____

City _____ State/Prov _____ Zip/Post Code _____

Phone _____ E-mail _____

Occupation _____ Position Held _____

Church _____

Pastor's Name _____

Church Position (if any)_____

CLASS 2 Attendance—Please Print

Name _____ Age _____ Date _____

Street Address _____

City _____ State/Prov _____ Zip/Post Code _____

Phone _____ E-mail _____

Occupation _____ Position Held _____

Church _____

Pastor's Name _____

Church Position (if any)_____

CLASS 3 Attendance—Please Print

Name _____ Age _____ Date _____

Street Address _____

City _____ State/Prov _____ Zip/Post Code _____

Phone _____ E-mail _____

Occupation _____ Position Held _____

Church _____

Pastor's Name _____

Church Position (if any)_____

ATTENDANCE SLIP

ATTENDANCE SLIP

ATTENDANCE SLIP

Memory Verse Cards

CARRY THESE CARDS WITH YOU
MEMORIZE EACH VERSE
REVIEW THE VERSES
SHARE THEM WITH OTHERS

Why memorize?

• To follow the example of Jesus Christ (Matthew 4:4, 7, 10). When tempted, He replied, "It is written," and quoted from the book of Deuteronomy.

• To control the thought life. "How can a young man keep his way pure? By living according to your word. . . . I have hidden your word in my heart that I might not sin against you" (Psalm 119:9, 11).

• To be equipped for service. "All Scripture is God-breathed and is useful for teaching, rebuking, correcting and training in righteousness, so that the man of God may be thoroughly equipped for every good work" (2 Timothy 3:16–17).

SEE OTHER SIDE FOR "HOW TO MEMORIZE"

Christ Is At The Door   *3*

"Here I am! I stand at the door and knock. If anyone hears my voice and opens the door, I will come in and eat with him, and he with me."

Revelation 3:20, NIV

We Must Receive Him   *3*

"Yet to all who received him, to those who believed in his name, he gave the right to become children of God"

John 1:12, NIV

Christ Paid The Penalty   *2*

"But God demonstrates his own love for us in this: While we were still sinners, Christ died for us."

Romans 5:8, NIV

Salvation A Free Gift   *2*

"For it is by grace you have been saved, through faith—and this not from yourselves, it is the gift of God—not by works, so that no one can boast."

Ephesians 2:8–9, NIV

People Are Sinful   *1*

"For all have sinned and fall short of the glory of God."

Romans 3:23, NIV

Sin Has A Penalty   *1*

"For the wages of sin is death, but the gift of God is eternal life in Christ Jesus our Lord."

Romans 6:23, NIV

How to Memorize

Memorize the Scriptures in the following order.

1. the topic   2. the verse   3. the reference

- The reference is often more difficult to remember than the verse; that is why it should be repeated before and after the verse. The reference is like the handle on a suitcase, enabling you to lift up from the Bible a complete portion whenever needed. As an aid, you will find the references printed on the cards to help you in reviewing your verses.

- The real secret of Scripture memory is review, review, review. "Either use it or lose it."

- Quote the verse aloud. Pray over the verse, asking God to make the meaning clear and applicable to you. Memorize one phrase at a time, using the reference, adding phrase by phrase until the entire verse is committed to memory.

We Must Receive Him   3

"But as many as received Him, to them He gave the right to become children of God, even to those who believe in His name."

John 1:12, NKJV

Salvation A Free Gift   2

"For by grace you have been saved through faith, and that not of yourselves; it is the gift of God, not of works, lest anyone should boast."

Ephesians 2:8–9, NKJV

Sin Has A Penalty   1

"For the wages of sin is death, but the gift of God is eternal life in Christ Jesus our Lord."

Romans 6:23, NKJV

Christ Is At The Door

"Behold, I stand at the door and kno If anyone hears My voice and opens door, I will come in to him and c with him, and he with Me."

Revelation 3:20, N

Christ Paid The Penalty

"But God demonstrates His own toward us, in that while we were sinners, Christ died for us."

Romans 5:8, N

People Are Sinful

"For all have sinned and fall shor the glory of God."

Romans 3:23, N